W9-CMQ-725

The River Styx, Ohio
and Other Poems

Also by Mary Oliver

No Voyage and Other Poems

The River Styx, Ohio
and Other Poems
by Mary Oliver

New York

Harcourt Brace Jovanovich, Inc.

Copyright © 1965, 1966, 1967, 1968, 1969, 1970,
1971, 1972 by Mary Oliver
All rights reserved. No part of this publication may be
reproduced or transmitted in any form or by any means,
electronic or mechanical, including photocopy, recording,
or any information storage and retrieval system,
without permission in writing from the publisher.
First edition
ISBN 0-15-177750-0
Library of Congress Catalog Card Number: 72-75420
Printed in the United States of America
B C D E

The author would like to thank the editors of the
following magazines, in which some of the poems in
this book were first printed: *The American Scholar,
American Weave, The Antioch Review, Chicago Review,
Chicago Tribune Magazine, Commonweal, The Literary
Review, The Midwest Quarterly, The Minnesota Review,
Mill Mountain Review, The New Republic, The New
York Times, Poet Lore, Prairie Schooner,* and
War/Peace Report.

811.54
O

EUCLID PUBLIC LIBRARY

MA-72- 25920

MAR 1 5 '73

For
My Mother and Father
and for
Molly Malone Cook

Contents

The River Styx, Ohio
and Other Poems

Stark Boughs on the Family Tree

Up in the attic row on row,
In dusty frames, with stubborn eyes,
My thin ancestors slowly fade
Under the flat Ohio skies.

And so, I think, they always were.
Like their own portraits, years ago
They paced the blue and windy fields,
Aged in the polished rooms below.

For name by name I find no sign
Of hero in this distant life,
But only men as calm as snow
Who took some faithful girl as wife,

Who labored while the drought, the flood
Crisscrossed the fickle summer air,
Who built great barns and propped their lives
Upon a slow heartbreaking care.

Why do I love them as I do,
Who dared no glory, won no fame?
In a harsh land that lies subdued,
They are the good boughs of my name.

If music sailed their dreams at all,
They were not heroes, and slept on,
As one by one they left the small
Accomplished, till the great was done.

Tom

It wasn't pleasant; yet there are worse things
Than someone standing softly in the dark
Tuned in to episodes of other lives.

After a while you might have said we had
A kind of understanding, as we called,
"Tom, Tom, where are you?" toward the shadowed trees.

His name, of course, was Tom only to us.
He had another, which he used to cross
The daylight (later a policeman spoke
That name; it settled strangely in our ears).

One day a neighbor found him in his car.
He must have come by night to make an end.
He left no message, was no one we knew
(Though someone said he grew up in these hills).

Now, with our privacy restored, we stroll
Freely across the lawns until we hear
Where something strikes against a twig or leaf.
What is it? Rabbit? Mouse? The sullen trees
Grow darker in their silence as we feel
Something that's much like (no, not terror) grief.

Hattie Bloom

She was, Grandfather said, *a fly-by-night,*
And did just what you'd guess her kind would do!
Listening behind the door, I thought of Hattie,
Who'd sailed the town trailing her silks like wings
And seemed to me as elegant and pale
As any night bird cruising in its feathers.
She'd made my uncle wild, that much I knew.
Though he was grown, he wept; though he was strong,
She taught him what it was to want and fail.

True to her kind! Grandfather said, and sneered.
A fly-by-night! Come to your senses, boy!
But it was months before my uncle turned
Back to the world, before his eyes grew mild;
And it was years before he loved again.
And what was I to think of such conclusions—
Pressed to the door, a small and curious child
Eavesdropping on the terrifying world
Of sons and fathers talking of their women?

I knew that Hattie Bloom had run away
The night before, gone like a gust of wind
On the night train, her perfumes like a veil
Left on the platform; and I knew somehow
The kind of life she lived—yet understood
That love, which made my gentle uncle wild,
Might also change a painted girl to gold.
The dream that smiled and trailed its silken wing
Was what my uncle grieved for; and I thought
The truth of love was that in truth, for him,
Lost Hattie Bloom became that perfect thing.

An Elegy for Hens

I was told of the beautiful horses
My grandfather used to keep,
Till their spirits swayed in the stables
And over the gardens of sleep.
But that was long ago;
By the time I was born and walking
And trailing my grandfather's shadow,
The horses were gone, and the barn
Converted to cages and pens
For a landscape of white hens.

What could I do with my dreams?
My grandfather laughed at the birds,
But I felt my life descending
To a clutter of eggs and straw.
And so it went on for years:
The horses tall in my sleep,
The squat hens pecking and jeering—
Until, with hardly a warning,
Nothing was left at all.

Now the barn is a house of webs
Where barn mice peer at the moon;
Silent arrives the morning,
Empty, the afternoon.
And in the black gardens of sleep
That hang above my bed,
The splendid hens come walking
And clap their wings, evoking
The laughter of the dead.

Spring in the Classroom

Elbows on dry books, we dreamed
Past Miss Willow Bangs, and lessons, and windows,
To catch all day glimpses and guesses of the greening
    wood lot,
Its secrets and increases,
Its hidden nests and kind.
And what warmed in us was no book-learning,
But the old mud blood murmuring,
Loosening like petals from bone sleep.
So spring surrounded the classroom, and we suffered to be
    kept indoors,
Droned through lessons, carved when we could with
    jackknives
Our pulsing initials into the desks, and grew
Angry to be held so, without pity and beyond reason,
By Miss Willow Bangs, her eyes two stones behind glass,
Her legs thick, her heart
In love with pencils and arithmetic.

So it went—one gorgeous day lost after another
While we sat like captives and breathed the chalky air
And the leaves thickened and birds called
From the edge of the world—till it grew easy to hate,
To plot mutiny, even murder. Oh, we had her in chains,
We had her hanged and cold, in our longing to be gone!
And then one day, Miss Willow Bangs, we saw you
As we ran wild in our three o'clock escape
Past the abandoned swings; you were leaning
All furry and blooming against the old brick wall
In the Art Teacher's arms.

Indian Pipes

I found them at last, on a hillside
Of laurel and pine, nobbing
From the brown earth with white bowls,
Tender: so wild, so close to home.

The longer I live the more I sense
Wilderness approaching; I used to walk
Miles to find wild things; now they find me,
Blossom under the very windows where
I am busy being grown up and tame.

I think it is more than chance, I think
It is a new kind of vision I have,
That a child, who must put wild things
In a mile by itself, could not bear.
I wake, wrapped in the town, knowing

The edges were only in my mind: all's one.
Indian pipes glisten, inches away.
While patience, charity rub at the cold frontier,
The seeds to everything drive through the air.

Alex

Where is Alex, keeper of horses?
Nobody knows.
He lived all year in the broken barn,
Dry summer stashed above the eaves.
Now that he's gone, who grieves, who can,
For Alex of the tangled beard?
The soiled old man,
He chased my brother once,
Waving a rusty gun,
And he had hungry eyes
For money and the bottle.

Last week the town officials
Came in their gleaming trucks
And tore his old barn down,
And the last horse was sold,
And he wasn't anywhere.
Well, maybe he's in the madhouse,
And maybe he's sleeping it off
Down at the edge of town,
Sprawled in a weedy bed,
Dreaming of horses and leather.

And maybe, with luck, he's dead.

On Being Caught under Some Trees
with My Notebook

No, no, for nothing,
Neither for love, nor your beauty,
Nor the stopping of pain,
Nor sleep, nor any desire,

I made this music in a dismal wood,
Stared where the clouds were stretched and thin
Like scratches in the morning sky,
And sun rose round and frail as glass
Among the twisted branches where the birds
Went wild with singing.
      I did not ask why.
It was some foolish reason. I am sure
There is a science that could make it plain.
I could go search the drums of fact, be done
With all the choirs of innocence that move
Like harps and timbrels through my wrists. No, no,

I have remembered beauty, for your life
Is stamped upon my spirit like a coin;
And I have loved, but in another place;
And I have wept, but at another hour;
And I have hungered, but it was not that.

I woke, and crossed the streets, and entered through
The heavy trees, not asking why the birds
Were wild, or why I am in love with pain,
Or where I am going, or why the words
Leaped through my heart like hounds. I only stood
And looked, a little while, at everything;
Until I had to run, or die, or sing.

A Country Gift

My grandmother used to leave a bowl of milk
At night on the back porch. I asked what came
To cool its thirst within that pool of china.
She only smiled, and would not give a name.
I used to stand in secret by the door,
Watching the darkness seep into the valley,
And always as the night came on I saw
Apparent things, but could not guess at more.
Was it some harmless cat, or some grim spirit—
Some wrinkled woodland god whose haunches leap
Past the world's boiling science—whose slack jowls
Lapped at the warm milk while we lay asleep?
Was it within the grip of rage or love
It prowled our yard and clambered up the stair
And found the gift of peace, the token there?
I never knew, and still I do not know.
But I remember how the thorned winds blow
Across the country dark, and how she said
It's better not to doubt or to offend
What we don't know of darkness and the soul—
As morning after morning we woke safe
And from the porch picked up an empty bowl.

Learning about the Indians

He danced in feathers, with paint across his nose.
Thump, thump went the drum, and bumped our blood,
And sent a strange vibration through the mind.
White Eagle, he was called, or Mr. White,

And he strutted for money now, in schoolrooms built
On Ohio's plains, surrounded by the graves
Of all of our fathers, but more of his than ours.
Our teachers called it Extracurricular.

We called it fun. And as for Mr. White,
Changed back to a shabby salesman's suit, he called it
Nothing at all as he packed his drums, and drove,
Tires screeching, out of the schoolyard into the night.

A Castle on the Danube

Surely truth is the universe of the very young;
Surely it belonged to us, a household of children
With so much time.
Or if I am wrong, consider those who sit
On lawns or in bedrooms assembling
The blue myth of childhood, the splendid
Passage of years combining to such leisure.
For three years before my grandmother died she sat
Imperial on the dark porch of summer
Recalling her life in a castle that bordered the Danube—
Who was two years old when she rode in her father's arms
To the edge of Ohio.
                              Say the old,
"I remember, I remember," but surely it is not any more
The truth they offer. For what, from those narrow files,
Would draw small listeners from the sun? Grandmother,
It was no harm, I think,
The way you called to us and, when we were gathered
Like a last fragile blessing,
Rowed us to that blue river,
Borrowed in your need another kingdom, and drew us
One by one through the mad castle door.

The Burial Ground

Under the cherry we buried them all—
Things furred and feathered Sally the cat brought home—
Till summer by summer she wearied, and under the cherry
We dug her a bed, and laid her down.

This morning—for the tree had long since fallen—
I worked to move the stump; its limp roots shook
And stirred the earth for yards around
Until at last the taproot broke.

I found nothing—and I had been afraid.
No bone of them, no rack of rib,
Or blank white skull,
Or backbone scattered in its lonely crib.

And also there, where Sally lay,
Was nothing—not a particle or sign.
Cleanly the dark earth tumbled through my fingers
When half a field away, like a fierce design,

Sally's grandson William leaped and missed
A bird that shook itself and flew away.
Bird and cat went through their motions slowly,
Like actors in a play.

The earth was cool and calm to touch,
And yet I felt the distant sun
Burning my shoulders as I dug
Where killed and killer rest as one,

And then dissolve. Running on light feet,
Young William came and nuzzled at my hand.
Some birds stopped near, and failed to see
Their shadows pressed against the land.

William curled to a nap; the birds
Flew on, with dark appointments set.
Only I, appalled at learning how
The crystals of the earth forget,

Turned in a circle in that place—
Looked backward years, and forward years:
A gift that sweetens brutal time,
And is the nightmare of our tears.

Night Flight

Traveling at thirty thousand feet, we see
How much of earth still lies in wilderness,
Till terminals occur like miracles
To civilize the paralyzing dark.

Buckled for landing to a tilting chair,
I think: if miracle or accident
Should send us on across the upper air,
How many miles, or nights, or years to go
Before the mind, with its huge ego paling,
Before the heart, all expectation spent,
Should read the meaning of the scene below?

But now already the loved ones gather
Under the dome of welcome, as we glide
Over the final jutting mountainside,
Across the suburbs tangled in their lights,

And settled softly on the earth once more
Rise in the fierce assumption of our lives—
Discarding smoothly, as we disembark,
All thoughts that held us wiser for a moment
Up there alone, in the impartial dark.

Inside

Outside, through fields and over other walls
That mark the less important boundaries,
Like ownership, or a place where roses grow,
Spring comes like a huge opossum

Out of the roots of the greening shag-trees,
Lumbering, yet with small
Delicate footsteps and a dog's primed nose,
To cuckold the civilized acres.

Inside, in our private garden,
We wander or sleep while the world grows bawdy—
The timid eloping, the farm boy in a shadow
Dreaming of young girls bathing in a meadow,
The farmer's wife baking the bread of the moon—

And then we laugh, for everything changes but us.
From our hillside of bricks and litter, we see it all:
The flowers and havoc, the beast that prowls at the wall.

While the farm boy runs away, and the sun goes down,
And the timid have babies under the risen moon,
We lie in a river of laughter, locked in our town,
And listen.

Thump, thump down the night
The old opossum in her bulky furs
Winds weeds along the walls, scratches the wards,
Cries that it can't be so,

But we know.
Dry from crown to toe,
We laugh when she cries,
And when she sings we cry,

And won't grow.

New England Houses

Said the old carpenters, "There was never much
We could count on. Weather, whiskey, girls
Warmed us for a while, then left us swamped or dry.
So we were happiest at our tasks of wood,
Shaped and hammered like disciples of time
Thinking, someday when we wake from an old man's sleep,
And there's no more women or whiskey, what
Will we dream of under the shifting weathers?"
So they drove the nails in straight and deep,
Pounding for love and a kind of salvation.
"Now," said the old carpenters, "the world
Has changed; the winds confuse our eyes;
Our thin arms reach in vain for boards;
The whiskey's gone, the women ghosts."
And time took them then, dry as sawdust,
And set them down among the uncut boards
That curl beneath the ground. But in our town
And the next, and the next, there are famous houses:
No matter how fierce the weather, they are warm and fast;
No matter the deaths of their owners—they last and they last.

The Juggler

When my father threw saucers into the air
And caught them spinning, one by one,
So rapidly the wheel seemed never broken,
We thought it was only for fun.

But the glazed faces of the saucers, and my father's hands
Moving like clockwork, and the lines of strain
Showing under his big laughter have stayed like a strange
    design
Of almost everything. Again and again

In my childhood I wept among the broken crockery:
My failure. I could not master the trick,
Could only practice and dream of spinning things
Up, up, till they vanished in the dark

And yet were safe, and would return again.
And so I have never lived like that, knowing
Myself to be adept and sure—
But, rather, in a wild disorder of coming and going:

Events, chapters, moments clear as glaze
With the big void still streaming around their faces
And my soul unconfident. Oh, graceful father,
I could not ever keep things in their places,

Like you, still stand here ankle deep in error,
Horrified when something spins away
Into the distance and settles
On some unreachable height. The game we played

A thousand miles, so many lawns away
Goes on, but it is not a game
Any more: the things I touch have breath and fire,
And what is broken moves me with a shame.

It is days and years; it is owing and loving,
Catching and scarcely holding and letting go
Object after object from my windmill arms, still dreaming
Of a skill I could never grow.

Sometimes it is wonderful: I do not falter for days.
Then, in the midst of ruin, shaking with pain,
I try to remember how tender you were with children,
How you swept up the wreckage, made us try it again.

Indian Lake

At Indian Lake my brother's face floated
Clear on the smooth blue surface of summer;
We waited for sunfish with rods of willow,
In skim-kneed concert we knelt together,
One young, one younger. The fish that rode by

Must be old and fat this later summer
I kneel to look for my brother's eyes,
Having looked all else where once he traveled.
But the fish are young and circled with rainbows,
The weeds they wind in are tender as cresses.

The skin of the lake holds a single image,
And space hangs calm beside this watcher,
Straight to some clouds, the deep, locked heavens.
Brother, I miss you. I find myself looking,
Sure you'd not sleep while the fish run so wild.

Forest and lakeside are young forever,
While time is our climate, which knows no returning.
Therefore we love, therefore we study despair.

At Indian Lake, brother, I found no sign
Of your whereabouts, or your loss; or any mention
That any person at all had ever been there.

Anne

The daughter is mad, and so
I wonder what she will do.
But she holds her saucer softly
And sips, as people do,
From moment to moment making
Comments of rain and sun,
Till I feel my own heart shaking—
Till I am the frightened one.
O Anne, sweet Anne, brave Anne,
What did I think to see?
The rumors of the village
Have painted you savagely.
I thought you would come in anger—
A knife beneath your skirt.
I did not think to see a face
So peaceful, and so hurt.
I know the trouble is there,
Under your little frown;
But when you slowly lift your cup
And when you set it down,
I feel my heart go wild, Anne,
I feel my heart go wild.
I know a hundred children,
But never before a child
Hiding so deep a trouble
Or wanting so much to please,
Or tending so desperately all
The small civilities.

Aunt Mary

Fat Aunt Mary, on my mother's side,
Weighed three hundred pounds, and maybe more.
The threshold trembled when she came to visit;
The hinges squealed on the kitchen door.
She sat in Papa's chair, while yards of gingham
Flowed away to hide her socks and shoes.
Her voice rolled through the farmhouse deep as thunder
When great Aunt Mary rumbled through the news.

How shall we guess the spirit that lies hidden?
Built like an ocean liner, wreathed in smiles,
The thing she loved the best was to go fishing,
To row alone over the liquid miles
And drop her line for perch and pike. It seemed
Incongruous then, but now I guess
She could recall a loveliness
Out there upon the blue and quiet waters
With nothing to be compared to but horizons.

But fat Aunt Mary was not always so—
In an old album idly looked at since
I stared to recognize a skinny child.
It was Mary, in a time before her glands
Grew wild as pumps, and fleshed her to a joke.
Remembering how she frightened all small children
As she loomed and puffed along the summer sand,
I tasted shame, and thought how wise we grow,
Just as the pulse of things slips from the hand
And we are left the empty cup of wish—
December it was, Aunt Mary carried seaward
Her last brave pound, caught her last lonely fish.

The Sanctuary

We all remember the cradle rocking,
And some of us, also, ourselves spilled out
Upon the roaring ground, while someone leaned
In horror over us—then stepped away
Into the shadows. And then, oh, then
The sanctuary is blasted, that never was!

Like something carved upon familiar stone
Turned innocently over one mild day,
A lingering information fastens me
Upon a darker wheel. No more, no more
A puppet dancing on the strings of habit,
I run beneath the trees. Now I have come

Into the loneliness of recognition;
And all who dare to walk without their strings
Enter the black abyss, the innless roads
Where love spelled out in rash complexities
Loses her summer look, and houses burn
Back to the hopeless, helpless myths they are.

And so forever the beautiful town
Disappears, fades like a pretty story
Or like an address blown by the wind away
From the book of the heart. Oh, it was neither
Castle nor mansion, but familiar house
Like any other on a slow mild street

Where aging people still, now, tend their dreams
Of how, in spite of all, it was to be;
Mumble their ancient theme of good intention
Among the accidents of awful harm;
And so, in innocence, still hope, and wait
For their dark sons and daughters to come home.

The Indians Visit the Museum

I wish they had come with drums and painted faces.
I wish they had come ornate and proud
And like a definition of wild places
Had merely stood erect before the crowd.

But the four old kings of the sleeping tribes
Must shake a thousand hands,
Must smile into a thousand cheerful faces
That profit from their blue and weedy lands.

Pride and pride only wins the careless heart:
No one listens this windy day
As the old lords talk on, begging for justice,
And smile in their defeat, and lope away.

Pre-Columbian now and labeled
Is all their cause and strife;
The curator leans among tomahawks and arrows,
Dreaming of his own life.

A Pine Woods Back of Town

Who are these boys, trespassing in the woods?
No one I know, they've slipped from the summer road
To sleep in leaves and moonlight. One lies curled
As though to huddle warmth in his Indian blanket;
The other lies sprawled out along the ground,
Cheek to the grass. It's more like an embrace,
Easy and willing. Pleased to keep their secret,
I left them, sleeping still, in that green place.

And if I could I would have stitched the leaves
Together for their sakes, for a safe keeping.
I was thinking of more than owners and their blunt anger.
I was thinking of wilder griefs a boy can come to—
The powers that cry alarm and hasten them over
Ocean, to darker woods, to darker purpose,
Where many, still in the conflicts of possession,
Are shaken from sleep, green forest, and the world.

Christmas, 1966

In the last of the Truro woods we find our tree;
The axe rings hollow through the leafless halls
Of winter, and the furred beast falls
Bouncing among the shrubs. We gather strings
Of squirrel corn, boughs of laurel. The crisp air
Rings with our voices, laughter. No one wonders
If Christ is here, if Christ is anywhere.

The steeples on the hills of Truro shine
As we ride home; faintly we can hear
The choirs in practice for the holy visit.
Like outlaws we will keep His festival
Without Him, pour the unblessed wine
Across our days and, knowing we are dead,
Be satisfied with loaves of human bread.

Under ten thousand decorated trees
The world is humming strands of Holy Night;
But only war, disaster, and disease
Shine in the patterns of the natural stars.
Christ is an old man in a church pew, weeping;
He waits, like common men, to glimpse the light.
Trying to make the best of it, we sit

Beneath the rough boughs of a lovely tree
And talk of love, of peace. But all the while
We dare to break through gravity and smile,
Something is shifting, like a deck of cards,
Or coal in Wales; we hear the explosions of cars,
Children in bedrooms stretch beneath nameless fevers;
Ships vanish in the rough wool of the sea.

Night Watch

We are sent to our stations, and go there,
And wait there, staring
At a green wall. I write this
Leaning among the leaves, the slow
Flavor of swamp everywhere, the salts
Of fear and fatigue on my clothes.
There is a bird. It cries in the dark.
It cries: when will the tree
Stop shaking, when will the nest hold
And the eggs hatch? And the nestlings cry
In great potbellied hunger, till they fly
And become the beautiful strangers, the riches
Of our neighborhood? The bird

Falls like a stone. O love, this is a letter
Of terrible desperation. We are soldiers, waiting,
Thinking of girls and half-woven nests
In small towns many months away, as easily lost

As here in the harbors of waiting a leaf, or a bird
Stirred from the limb of sleep to beat its wings
In a dream of peace, in the zones of holocaust.

The Nightingale

Once in London I heard
Faintly and for a moment only
A nightingale; it was April
And Keats a hundred years dead.

It is a memory scarcely worth
Repeating, for as I said the bird
Was far away, and scarcely heard—
And yet I leaned for hours that night
Over the sill, into the plane trees' leaves,
Thinking of Keats and how we all,
Like birds that have flown, make distance firm,

How hard it is to keep life warm,

Glad, glad of a little word.

The Fence

The day the fence was finally in
And I could see to every side
The wire that glittered fierce and thin,
The sturdy posts among the leaves,
I felt a curious change begin
To whisper slyly in my heart
That things were different on my side,
Were cleaner and more civilized
Than the green portions running free.
And though I knew it could not be,
Since only days before I'd walked
Under the trees and could not tell
What leaves were wild, and which were mine,
I felt the notion rise and flare
Like heat about my willing pride.

Who builds a fence about his land
Must bear the burden of those lines,
And lest the sharp whim of a fence
Create a myth of difference,
Teach love to leap, respect to glide
Oh freely to the other side.
For there's no wilderness but one,
And no safe place for any life
That fear or fencing ever won.

Under the green and falling light
I walk the borders of my land
And let my thoughts swim into night;
And pray that they should travel far,
Look to the earth both here and there,
Study the wild unpastured stars,
Stare at the dark no fence can hold
And, finally, leave the gate ajar.

Mr. Frost's Chickens

He did not love them,
Nor they him.
As chickens go, they were chickens,
Plotting for social position, dreaming of grain.
The eggs came as afterthoughts—
Though not to Mr. Frost,
Counting up the cost of the grain they clucked for.

When things go wrong, I think of Mr. Frost
And his flock of chickens,
And the poems that were lost, maybe,
While he shoveled coops,
Picked eggs,
Threw grain.

Fame was years away.
Health not improved by the hours that one must keep
When one keeps chickens.
Eggs sparse.
I say, on a bad day,
Everybody has something.
Thank you, Mr. Frost, for the chilly interval
Of chicken farming.

Answers

If I envy anyone it must be
My grandmother in a long ago
Green summer, who hurried
Between kitchen and orchard on small
Uneducated feet, and took easily
All shining fruits into her eager hands.

That summer I hurried too, wakened
To books and music and circling philosophies.
I sat in the kitchen sorting through volumes of answers
That could not solve the mystery of the trees.

My grandmother stood among her kettles and ladles.
Smiling, in faulty grammar,
She praised my fortune and urged my lofty career.
So to please her I studied—but I will remember always
How she poured confusion out, how she cooled and labeled
All the wild sauces of the brimming year.

The Intervals

A skirmish in the mountains.
After planting, after supper, we are told
The shape of the battle, the sum of the dead.
Only the details are new; the rest is so old

It reads like the book of another time,
A fever passed down, passed down, that we must bear
Like the shape of our bones. There are certain
Beetles, and dry winds, that spin through the air

Passing some farms and eating up others.
It is the possible claw that crawls our sleep,
But lightly: we are used to it.
It does not make us shout or weep.

Thus war now, in its age. Between crises.
This is the worst of it, that on the green hills
A few more die each day, and we can bear it.
Like the very wind and weather, the worn bells toll.

The Esquimos Have No Word for "War"

Trying to explain it to them
Leaves one feeling ridiculous and obscene.
Their houses, like white bowls,
Sit on a prairie of ancient snowfalls
Caught beyond thaw or the swift changes
Of night and day.
They listen politely, and stride away

With spears and sleds and barking dogs
To hunt for food. The women wait
Chewing on skins or singing songs,
Knowing that they have hours to spend,
That the luck of the hunter is often late.

Later, by fires and boiling bones
In steaming kettles, they welcome me,
Far kin, pale brother,
To share what they have in a hungry time
In a difficult land. While I talk on
Of the southern kingdoms, cannon, armies,
Shifting alliances, airplanes, power,
They chew their bones, and smile at one another.

Points of View

When the bullet nicks but does not kill,
Or the shrapnel stops but does not shear,
A man may live a life of chairs,
Harness and hooks and willow limbs.
It is better than the lonely grave.

And anyway it's not so rare
As it once was. Whole troops of men,
Some portion lacking, slip away
To towns and countryside, too glad
For life to rage for what's not there.

And anyway there is such cheer
In factories where the leather and the tree
Take on the tender shape of hands,
Or legs, or feet, or muscled arms.
There soldiers go to be made whole.

And if somewhere beyond those fine new factories
Someone should cry out *cause and effect,* and weep
Like a man who has fallen in dream, oh, who will hear
Over the tools and smiles of the clever technicians
Carving so beautifully willow hands and feet?

The Survival

Hand in hand beside the shattered plane,
They dressed their wounds and wove a leafy bed,
And four days later woke in the cold leaves
To hear the search plane banking overhead.

Back home and famous in their snug apartment,
He tells the brief adventure to their friends.
She listens—combed, serene—and neither mentions
How year by year the salt of things descends,

Or how they woke together in the forest
To find their lives, like chill repeating dreams,
Warmed by fear's excitement—and like children
Broke through the ice and drank from summer's streams.

Sometimes, in years to come, he will remember
Leaves in her hair and berries in her hand;
In a white bed she dreams of that wild brother
Glimpsed for a moment in an impossible land.

The Transients

Unsatisfied with things as they are,
Sooner or later you see them stand
In the cool of the evening, drinking in
The silence of the distant land;

And sooner or later you hear the sound
Of doors being opened and flung shut—
The whir of the car in the dead of the night,
As they gather their trifles and move out.

I think they find no better world.
Yet, leaning through the boneless dark
To watch their lights slide down the road,
I wish all travelers good luck.

For I remember days I too
Have scorned these streets of greed and grief,
Have looked across the sky and felt
The flash of possible relief;

Have dreamed I too might leave behind
This painful and irrational scene—
And stood whole mornings gazing on
Distance, that always seems serene.

Isabel Sparrow

Isabel Sparrow, who is she?
Brought up in conversation and put down,
A thin sweet woman flashed upon the air
And vanished through the haze of a lost town.

Was it a hundred years or two she walked
In her tidy leather shoes?
Did she find love, bear children? Questions press
Hard to my heart, leaving a curious bruise.

For no one can tell, no one remembers or wonders
Or even is certain why
Her name came up, like a drifting leaf, to be spoken
And casually passed by.

Isabel Sparrow, fate grants us no quarter,
Flashes your faint blue smile, and then no more.
It is enough—at night I hear the sea wind
Blowing and blowing through your vanished door.

A Walk from the Asylum

The gate swung closed; this time I was outside.
Among the trees the path wound round and round
Until I understood that one of us
Was hiding from the other; but at last
I found the village and a little shop
Where they sold meats and things, and went inside.

The butcher said good morning. I replied.
We talked some more and then he wrapped in paper
Two plump wild kidneys and two dripping hearts.
I paid the dollar and got back some change.
The cat? he said. I answered him, the cat.
Do you like cats? he said. I said nothing.
It was a thing I never could decide.

He turned away to serve somebody else
And I went back along the winding land
Because I lived up there, locked on the hill.
It is not true caught things strive to be free—
There is a thing that battles for the dark.
The package cried and throbbed till I grew mad
To leave it in some field, to let it be.

And so how long it took, I cannot say.
Perhaps the sun went down, perhaps I died
To things a while. But in reality
I think the space was small that seemed so wide.
I only know I saw the gate swing open
And knew that they had opened it for me.
I only know I entered in, one day,
Burdened with violence, but walking mild—
And was no more of their society.

Encounter

I lift the small brown mouse
Out of the path and hold him.
He has no more to say,
No lilt of feet to run on.
He's cold, still soft, but idle.
As though he were a stone
I launch him from my hand;
His body falls away
Into the shadowed wood
Where the crackling leaves rain down,
Where the year is mostly over.
"Poor creature," I might say,
But what's the use of that.
The clock in him is broken.
And as for ceremony,
Already the leaves have swirled
Over, the wind has spoken.

O Pioneers

Headed through wilderness to found a nation,
They dreamed of farms and easy sleep,
And kept their powder dry, and talked with God,
And shed the cloth of England for the buckskin,
And carved new habits for their sons to keep.

Yea, for the Lord's sake, and for their unborn sons,
They strode across the continent, and took
The rivers and the forest and the prairie
And spun them into farms, and bore strong children
Between the musket and the old prayer book.

Maybe in earth, shaped into roots, they lie.
Or maybe, met in Heaven with their sons,
Lean down, peer back, to where America
Glitters and roars and suffers what she is—
A land built step by step with God and guns.

Resistance

Now earth turns over, breaking at the root
All green, all easily established things.
We resist, or we die.

I think we thought that peace would last forever.
We were mistaken. Braced against the wind,
Wounded, confused, inadequate, we stand
And watch the gifts of the green seasons drift
Over a hardening land.

Who dream of perfection surely invite this day.
Leaves fall, opening terrible vistas.
Birds cry into the wind, and flap away.

They will come again. We will endure. But nothing,
Nor time nor healing,
Can lead us back to where we thought we were.

Passing Through

One after one the white towns fall away,
Our entrance and departure barely stirring
The leaves upon the trees that shelter lawns
Leading to other doors and lives, not ours.
Bright for a moment, hung within the eyes,
Strange landscapes almost touch the mind, and then,
One after one the passing miles are gone.

The world begins with something realized,
And all we see is what we care to see;
And so it is, and so it long shall be
On every journey that is merely time:
Over our speeding shoulders, day by day,
Great structures fade beneath the autumn air
As though they never happened, never were.

And wilderness and longing, they remain.

All that men know is what they dare to treasure.
And so for years, over the random highways,
We make our small arrivals and depart;
And the high cities of the green earth echo
The dark that rules the country of the heart.

Squire's Castle

She was afraid of wilderness, and so
He built a castle firm against the leaves
Of harsh Ohio. But its thick walls crumble
In empty rooms, and casual water flows

Into the hall. They say the lovers parted—
She home to England, he to wilder lands
Westward of that green slope where tourists wonder
Why a cold castle stands

On the small hills above the curving river,
Where boys and girls come in their modern cars
Deep in the night, and shyly wander
In and out the mossy doors.

The wind has rubbed for years along the granite,
But still the desolation is not calm.
Nervous, the youngsters touch across the darkness,
And flee the stones that never were a home.

Poor Sir, I think of how your frenzy balanced
Stone upon stone, to hide the swollen moon.
Poor Lady, how you must have feared the winters,
Hearing, beyond his smile, the owl's dark tune.

The thickest wall cannot keep out the forest.
Your folly, Sir, is fading in the trees:
A warning to the young who look for shelter
To build their house of air, of sheerest leaves.

Elegy for Five Fishermen

Widows of the sea, light many candles,
And forgive us our new voyages,
Our voices loud in the distance
Still talking of profits and fathoms.

Five men drowned on a sunny day,
And a dozen christian towns away
We crown the defeat with another,
Unable, as always, to weep for a mere idea.

For when other men die, from other houses,
We put on solemn faces and we say,
"Tragic but passing, tragic but passing";
And scarcely feel the sudden lurch and sway

Of the long waves as we glide to safe landing—
Scarcely notice the difference at all
Along the torn coast of good fortune
Where we are still standing.

The Islands

That was the year we planned to go,
Bundling the children and a few belongings
Onto the southbound ship. We'd dreamed for years
Of yellow sand and friendly dark-haired dancers.
What happened then—what made us hesitate?
Why did we think it might be better later?
Here in a northern suburb where the snow
Clings to the earth and drifts along the roads,
We work and clap our hands against the cold.
Not having dreams or failures to outlive,
The children seem to like it where they are.
And as for us, that hot and fragrant shore
Has faded, if it has not dropped away.
The harbor is a place of ice and cargo.
The tall ships we believed in, in our heyday,
Have gone, and do not stop here any more.

Somewhere in Pennsylvania

Somewhere in Pennsylvania when the stars
Like blossoms just started to close
And I must have been tired the last
Long miles, I saw

Two people just like us,
But younger and doing fine, darling, doing
All the right things, walking

Ahead of me down the road. And then
One of them turned and it was you,
And I must have been tired but only a length
Of the simple road between us and so I

Hurried, I hurried not to lose you
A second time. And then the cruiser
Forced me to the shoulder, and the cop

Who has seen everything, darling, said,
"Mister, if you did
Ninety all night, in any
Direction whatsoever, you couldn't catch up."

The Garden

She kept three gardeners. Nevertheless, at night,
Her heart could hear the lopped vines crawling back
Over the lawn and up the gravel walk—
Could hear the fences groan with their looped weight,

And was afraid. By day she kept
The three men busy; clippers, mowers, rakes
Helped her to keep the wilderness at bay.
But still at night she felt the grassy lakes

Put out new roots and move, the tender boughs
Of the cut hedges squirming out of line.
So, through the polished windows of her years,
She watched the sure collapse of her design,

Stared at the moon defeated, and grew cold
To learn at last how powerless she was.
For all her wealth, good manners, and defiance,
She lived alone in a surrounded house

And like the least of us grew old and weedy,
Felt her mind crumble like a wall of stones,
Heard the trees thicken as they stumbled toward her
And set their cracking weight upon her bones.

Mountain Road

My grandfather kept no
Unicorns in his grey barn,
But hurly-burly slant-eyed goats
That nimbled through the stacks of hay
And filled the milk pails every day.

My grandmother kept in her scriptures
No potions drained from the moon,
Kept no recipes in her grey head
To change the shape of men or wolves.
But I remember on her shelves
Apple butter and new bread.

Enchantment is a distant time.
Their farm was recent, filled with truth,
With buttered bread and milk in bowls,
And he and she were simple souls.
And yet I say, in all the earth
I have not found a place so sweet.

So it may be some charm did lay
Its arm across their small estate.
In any case when it dissolved—
Sank with their age into the wind
And woods again—we found it was
A story time could not repeat.

72— 25920

The Ceremony

Now in the law and order of a death,
I feel the desolation of the living
Led through some wilderness; however fitting
Or inappropriate to the mute dead,
I feel loose grief confined and bolted down
As we ride forth in black and polished mourning,
Bells drag the wind above the civil town.

There is a place men go to keep the dead:
To the locked buildings where no custom rules,
Where men like children sleep and shield their visions—
But nothing's brave or peaceful in such schools.
Wherefore this day we fill up hollow time
With ancient regulations, and we move
Under the bells, among the crepe and lilies,
Mere symbols of our station and our love.

Above the terrible, the cherished dead,
Our hearts, whirling with random shadows, lean
Imagining the trick of our own doom;
Our minds stand ready at the edge of chaos—
Till ceremony turns us from the room.

Magellan

Like Magellan, let us find our islands
To die in, far from home, from anywhere
Familiar. Let us risk the wildest places,
Lest we go down in comfort, and despair.

For years we have labored over common roads,
Dreaming of ships that sail into the night.
Let us be heroes, or, if that's not in us,
Let us find men to follow, honor-bright.

For what is life but reaching for an answer?
And what is death but a refusal to grow?
Magellan had a dream he had to follow.
The sea was big, his ships were awkward, slow.

And when the fever would not set him free,
To his thin crew, "Sail on, sail on!" he cried.
And so they did, carried the frail dream homeward.
And thus Magellan lives, although he died.

The Wall

A few leaves leaning forward strike the window—
Maples, of a heavy forest, where birds float shy
And bright as beads. The hills beyond, ascending,
Channel the winds and shut off half the sky.

Dearest, as we wake to another morning,
I think of all the years and all the schools
Bent toward the civilizing of our spirits,
I think of all the lectures and the rules,

The lives of governors, the laws of Euclid
Laid on our minds and fastened down,
All the while birds dashed in their hungry circles,
Vines churned along the edges of the town.

Dearest, though we have promised to care forever,
Remember, beyond these rooms where we sleep and wake,
It is green as jungle, singing, corruptible;
And the wall is a lie that any wind could break.

Going to Walden

It isn't very far as highways lie.
I might be back by nightfall, having seen
The rough pines, and the stones, and the clear water.
Friends argue that I might be wiser for it.
They do not hear that far-off Yankee whisper:
How dull we grow from hurrying here and there!

Many have gone, and think me half a fool
To miss a day away in the cool country.
Maybe. But in a book I read and cherish,
Going to Walden is not so easy a thing
As a green visit. It is the slow and difficult
Trick of living, and finding it where you are.

A Walk Through the Graveyard

Now as the cold November wind
Sweeps against the matted hills,
I walk where the crackling weathers shake
The many birds, the manifold leaves,
And try to find a thing that grieves
To hear the cloth of snow come on,
To hear the panting, boneless step
Of death that waits to take the world—
And learn how nothing, nothing cares.
To the tree, the river, the dreamless hill
That have spilled their seed and fruit away,
Death is the brimming of the cup,
Time's simple and most natural close.

Though it is easier not to dream,
To bother as the hard years fall,
To take no friend or hope or brother,
How will we know that we have lived
In a world apart from leaves and wind?
The rich who give their days to toys,
The proud who cannot learn to break,
The greedy with no hearts at all
Will win the tinsels of the earth
And rot in tunnels soft as snow.
Those alone, who took the chance
And practiced love, and dared despair,
Will never fall from shapes of grace;
Those alone, who came to care
The way it was with other lives,
Have struggled above rock and beast,
Have set their grain against the rest,
And, beautiful as trees still green,
Argue the winter of this place.

The River Styx, Ohio

We drove through October, Grandmother pointing at cows;
Mother, bifocaled, squinting at maps for a crossroad.
We came instead to the River Styx, Ohio.

Dead leaves fell ruffling like an ugly lace
Down the brown hillsides, past some empty buildings.
We left the car and wandered through a field,
Three ladies pausing in indifferent space.

Some cows drank from a creek, and lurched away.
Whoever named the place learned the hard lesson,
I'd guess, without much fanfare or delay.
Farms to both sides shook, bankrupt, in the wind.

We hope for magic; mystery endures.
We look for freedom, but the measure's set.
There was a graveyard, but we saw no people.
We went back to the car.

Dim with arthritis, time, the muddied seasons,
Grandmother poised in the back seat again,
Counting the cows. My mother's tightening fingers
Scratched at the roads that would take us home. On the wheel
I tensed my knuckles, felt the first stab of pain.

MAR 15 '73

73
77
81

Ma72-25920   811.54-O

OLIVER, MARY J.
   THE RIVER STYX, OHIO, AND OTHER
POEMS.

Ma72-25920   811.54-O

OLIVER, MARY J.
   THE RIVER STYX, OHIO AND OTHER
POEMS.

72

EUCLID PUBLIC LIBRARY

MAIN LIBRARY

631 E. 222nd Street
Euclid, Ohio 44123

261-5300

PLEASE DO NOT REMOVE
CARD FROM THIS POCKET